EASY INSTRUMENTAL DUETS

MW00559041

HIT SONGS FOR TWO

Arrangements by Peter Deneff

ISBN 978-1-5400-1282-1

HAL•LEONARD®

7777 W. BLUEMOUND RD. P.O. BOX 13819 MILWAUKEE, WI 53213

Visit Hal Leonard Online at
www.halleonard.com

CONTENTS

ALL ABOUT THAT BASS

CELLOS

Words and Music by KEVIN KADISH
and MEGHAN TRAINOR

ALL OF ME

CELLOS

Words and Music by JOHN STEPHENS
and TOBY GAD

BRAVE

CELLOS

Words and Music by SARA BAREILLES
and JACK ANTONOFF

BUDAPEST

CELLOS

Words and Music by GEORGE BARNETT
and JOEL POTT

CAN'T STOP THE FEELING

from TROLLS

CELLOS

Words and Music by JUSTIN TIMBERLAKE,
MAX MARTIN and SHELLBACK

GRENADE

CELLOS

Words and Music by BRUNO MARS,
ARI LEVINE, PHILIP LAWRENCE,
BRODY BROWN, CLAUDE KELLY
and ANDREW WYATT

Moderately

HEY, SOUL SISTER

CELLOS

Words and Music by PAT MONAHAN,
ESPEN LIND and AMUND BJORKLUND

HOME

CELLOS

Words and Music by GREG HOLDEN
and DREW PEARSON

I WILL WAIT

CELLOS

Words and Music by
MUMFORD & SONS

Slightly slower

LET HER GO

CELLOS

Words and Music by
MICHAEL DAVID ROSENBERG

LET IT GO

CELLOS

Words and Music by JAMES BAY
and PAUL BARRY

100 YEARS

CELLOS

Words and Music by
JOHN ONDRASIK

POKER FACE

CELLOS

Words and Music by STEFANI GERMANOTTA
and RedOne

ROYALS

CELLOS

Words and Music by ELLA YELICH-O'CONNOR
and JOEL LITTLE

(small note optional)

SAY SOMETHING

CELLOS

Words and Music by IAN AXEL,
CHAD VACCARINO and MIKE CAMPBELL

SHAKE IT OFF

CELLOS

Words and Music by TAYLOR SWIFT,
MAX MARTIN and SHELLBACK

SHAPE OF YOU

CELLOS

Words and Music by ED SHEERAN,
KEVIN BRIGGS, KANDI BURRUSS,
TAMEKA COTTLE, STEVE MAC
and JOHNNY McDAID

Moderately fast

SKYFALL

from the Motion Picture SKYFALL

CELLOS

Words and Music by ADELE ADKINS
and PAUL EPWORTH

SOME NIGHTS

CELLOS

Words and Music by JEFF BHASKER,
ANDREW DOST, JACK ANTONOFF
and NATE RUESS

STAY WITH ME

CELLOS

Words and Music by SAM SMITH,
JAMES NAPIER, WILLIAM EDWARD PHILLIPS,
TOM PETTY and JEFF LYNNE

STORY OF MY LIFE

CELLOS

Words and Music by JAMIE SCOTT,
JOHN HENRY RYAN, JULIAN BUNETTA,
HARRY STYLES, LIAM PAYNE, LOUIS TOMLINSON,
NIALL HORAN and ZAIN MALIK

VIVA LA VIDA

CELLOS

Words and Music by GUY BERRYMAN,
JON BUCKLAND, WILL CHAMPION
and CHRIS MARTIN